Response Ability

IN THE CLASSROOM

Your Thoughts, Your Thinking, Your Choice

Written by Teachers for Teachers
Cyndi Willmarth and Paige Brown

ISBN: 979-8-9991733-0-0

For permissions, contact:
Cyndi Willmarth and Paige Brown
C&P Publishing
www.theresponseabilityproject.com

This is a work of nonfiction. While every effort has been made to ensure the accuracy of the information presented, this book is not intended to serve as professional, medical, or therapeutic advice. The content reflects the authors' personal experiences and perspectives and is not intended to represent or prescribe the experiences of others. Readers are encouraged to seek guidance from qualified professionals when making decisions related to their personal or professional lives.

Printed in the United States of America

First Edition: 2025

Contents

Preface

Dear Educator,

You've chosen to read this book, and we are *so* glad you have. Like you, we know what it's like to be a classroom teacher because we've been there too. Together, we have over fifty years of classroom experience and have had the incredible opportunity to work with hundreds of children, their families, and fellow educators. So yes, we *do* understand what it's like to be deeply committed to this work and also completely exhausted by it. That's exactly why we finally sat down to put what we've learned in writing. This book is truly our gift to you.

This is a book by teachers, for teachers. After years of reflection and endless conversations, we felt a deep stirring to share what we've discovered about creating and staying grounded in a joyful classroom. Not because everything was calm and conflict free (conflict is inevitable) but because we learned how to work with it and how to see it. We want to let you in on this, too.

Let's start by being real with you: this is a book about social-emotional development, classroom management, discipline, and guidance. Yes, all of those things. If you've ever read a book or attended a training on any of these topics, you know how much they overlap. The terms might differ slightly, but at the heart of it all, we're asking the same question: How do we get these students to stop driving us crazy, listen, follow directions, and just get along with each other? Right? Because honestly, wouldn't teaching be so much easier if kids just knew how to behave?

Well, guess what? We believe we can help ease that tension you carry home in your shoulders and settle the swirl in your mind. **But** unlike many SEL trainings you've attended, this isn't about *changing* children.

We're not here to tell you how to "get kids to do" anything.

What we are going to talk about is *you* and what happens when you choose to practice what we explore in this small book. And here's the incredible part: when you do, children may begin to show you something new. They may even start to transform before your eyes. Why? Because the way you see what's happening in front of you will start to change. You might even begin to see all those challenges as opportunities. Yes, really. It's amazing.

Here's the truth: teachers are social beings, operating from emotional brains. And children come to you with the same kind of brains. As much as we'd love to believe there's a magic trick to make children compliant so they can learn...there just isn't. Just as there's no magic spell that turns you into Mary Poppins for your administrator.

Behavior change is an inside job for children, and for you.

The more you embrace this idea and begin to explore your own lens, how you view what's happening around you, the more peace you'll feel and the more power you'll have in choosing how to respond. If there's any magic in teaching, that's it.

And here's one more thing: this work doesn't stop with the children in your classroom. It reaches into your relationships with co-teachers, administrators, and families, too. The same practices that help you connect with kids can help you navigate the adult dynamics that shape your day. Because the heart of this work...self-awareness, empathy, and presence, isn't just for teaching. It's for living.

And here's the incredible part: when you begin to shift how you engage with presence, awareness, and intention, things around you may begin to shift as well. Children may show you something new. Relationships might feel less strained. Even the hardest moments might start to look a little different.

Why? Because how you *see* what's happening changes. And when that changes, so does everything else.

You may begin to see challenges as invitations. You may find possibility where there used to be pressure. And yes, you may even begin to feel a little more like yourself again.

This book is small but mighty. You can read it in one sitting and there's value in that. However, we encourage you to take it in bite-sized bits; That's how we wrote it.

Read one chapter at a time, and give yourself space to reflect. Take a moment with the questions we ask and maybe keep a journal. Then, go back and read it again.

We also wrote it with intentional breaks between certain phrases and sentences. That was on purpose to provide you with the opportunity to take a deep breath and reflect on what you just read; We are sure the words will resonate with you at a deep level.

Highlight the lines that stand out. Write in the margins. And if you can, share what you've discovered with a co-worker or friend. Even better, read it together.

Finally, from the bottom of our hearts: thank you. Thank you for everything you do, every single day. It's impossible to fully explain to someone who hasn't taught what the experience is really like. But we know. And we are deeply grateful for your choice to show up and climb into the joyful trenches. You are not alone.

Best wishes to you as you embrace your newfound **response** *ability*.

You've got this.

Let's GO!

Cyndi and Paige

Acknowledgments

We want to take a moment to express our deepest gratitude to the people, moments, and innovations that made this book possible. Without them, this journey would not have been the same.

To Our Students:

First and foremost, we want to thank the hundreds of children who walked through our classroom doors over the years. Your presence gave us the chance to seek, learn, and practice everything we share in these pages. You are the heart of this work. You are the reason we searched for a different way, and discovered the power of human connection, nurturing social-emotional environments, and *looking within* for understanding. Thank you for allowing us the privilege of being part of your learning and growth. We are forever grateful.

To Our Mentor, Dr. Becky Bailey:

While many researchers, philosophers, teachers and authors have shaped our path, one in particular holds a special place in our hearts: Dr. Becky Bailey, founder of Conscious Discipline. More than 25 years ago, she introduced us to the life-changing idea that social-emotional development in the classroom begins with the adults. Her bold and compassionate teachings, especially the truth that *"no one can make you mad without your permission"* ignited a spark in us. It reshaped how we saw ourselves, our students, and our role as educators. For your vision, your courage, and your unwavering belief in the power of connection, we thank you, Dr. Bailey.

To Our Friends and Family:

We are endlessly grateful to our friends and family who patiently listened as we shared stories and insights from the classroom. Your encouragement gave us the space and grace to practice what we were learning, not just professionally, but personally. You reminded us that true growth in understanding connection, decision-making, and accountability begins with us, the adults. Thank you for being our sounding boards and cheerleaders through it all.

To Technology and Modern Tools:

We also want to acknowledge the technological advances that helped bring this book to life. Video conferencing platforms allowed us to meet and write together, even from 4,400 miles and an ocean apart. Artificial Intelligence lent a hand in creating the graphics, editing, and formatting, making the process smoother and more accessible. Online self-publishing platforms provided a way for us to share this work with the world in a manageable and empowering way. For all of this, we are incredibly grateful.

We hope that fellow educators will take their experiences, learnings, and stories from the classroom and also share them with the world. After all, experience is life's greatest teacher, and the wisdom of those who practice daily in real classrooms is a gift that deserves to be shared.

Introduction

A Story from the Classroom

It was a Tuesday morning. The drive into work was uneventful, there was no holiday coming up in the near future, and all of the students showed up that day. Just a typical Tuesday morning and the weekend loomed far off in the distance. And actually... so did I.

Even though my body was firmly planted at a circle time rug, my mind was miles away, thinking about my Spring Break and the days when I would sit and read quietly in my beach chair without a care in the world. I sipped on my cold coffee and began the circle time where no one was actually sitting crisscross applesauce **or** in a circle...when it happened. One child pushed another and cried "She's looking at me!" Tears. Yelling. Instant confusion. And in the middle of it, I could feel the fire rising in me.

I wanted to shout, *"Stop it right now! This is ridiculous. Are we really doing this AGAIN!"* I wanted to scream, *"Seriously?! We JUST talked about gentle hands!"* My body was doing that thing...heat in my face and tension in my chest. My nervous system screaming: **DO SOMETHING.**

I glanced up at the behavior chart I had on the wall... the chart that had fourteen little "pots of gold" each with a different number of gold coins in it, based on the times I had caught them "being good." I opened my mouth to say, "If you don't stop this right now, your pot of gold is getting dumped."

But somewhere in the swirl of it all, I caught this tiny flicker of awareness. A whisper in my brain that said:

"Let's do this differently."

So instead of reacting, I paused. Just for a second…but it was enough. Enough to change what I did next. I grounded myself. I took a breath (yes, even in the noise), and reminded myself:

"Be here now. This isn't personal. No one is in danger. I am fine. They are fine. Let's see what I can teach in this moment that might be helpful."

I looked up and around and saw the few uninvolved, and probably now anxious, children watching me. The assistant teacher was giving me that frustrated and "here we go again" look.

I softened my face. I leaned in calmly and said, "Oh friends, it looks like something happened here. Let's all take a deep breath together and see if we can figure something out.

In that brief, deliberate pause, everything seemed to still and I made the conscious choice to stay present, focused, and intentional in both my words and actions.

Was it perfect? No. Was everyone happy afterwards? Probably not.

But was it **conscious**?

Yes. I actually remember thinking "Let's do this differently." And that changed everything; It actually felt better. Because the real power is in that tiny little pause. In that moment you create the opportunity for responsive and resilient choice. In recognition that there is always a better way. A way that aligns with *your* truth and your intention and your values.

When you pause on purpose, you remember: You always have a choice in how you respond.

You have the ability to respond. And in that response is your peace and empowerment. You hold the **response ability**.

You Deserve This...

This book was born out of hundreds of moments like that...moments we lived, reflected on together, and now share with you.

Moments where we would feel like we were about to fall apart or snap or give up and walk out (yes, we know you've had those moments too) but instead, something shifted inside and we knew from somewhere deep within, there's another way.

And in that shift, we created an intentional and conscious pause. We caught our breath and used it to regulate ourselves and then noticed that space to choose.

From those small pauses, new responses emerged. From new responses, new patterns of response developed. And from those patterns, empowerment, confidence, and peace: a closer alignment to our true selves.

As Carl Jung, a psychiatrist whose work bridged psychology and philosophy, once reflected,

"The privilege of a lifetime is to become who you truly are."

His exploration of self-actualization and individuation speaks to the very heart of what it means to pause, reflect, and align with your true self. And that journey, the one toward your most grounded, conscious, and intentional self, begins with one conscious and tiny pause at a time.

This isn't a book about fixing yourself. It's not here to pile more onto your already overflowing to-do list. You've got enough on your plate. Instead, this is about taking what's already inside you… your wisdom, your experience, and your heart, and learning how to use it in a new way. A conscious way. A grounded, growth-oriented, and empowered way.

You're not just teaching children how to count or read or share. You're teaching them how to live, fully and courageously and with empathy, presence, and purpose.

You're teaching them how to navigate big feelings, how to repair when things go wrong, and how to stay connected even in conflict. You're showing them what it looks like to be human…Not perfect, but present. Not always calm but always coming back to center. And that? That is life changing.

And the way you handle your own stress, frustration, conflict, and overwhelm? *That* is the real curriculum. Not the kind that comes prepackaged in a box or binder, but the one that unfolds moment by moment.

These are the everyday, real-life lessons that matter most because they're authentic, meaningful, and grounded in what's actually happening right in front of you.

You are the foundation of your students' social-emotional learning. And let's face it, there are multitudes of times and experiences every day for real life lessons for them. But those times and experiences are also *for* you. *You deserve this.*

You deserve to feel the peace and strength that comes from knowing you have a choice. You are not a victim of your circumstances, you are the *author* of how each moment unfolds. You deserve to spend your days joyfully, intentionally, on purpose, and mindfully present...

Not just counting down to the weekend or wishing for spring break but saying and believing "I really love my job, this work matters deeply, and this is exactly what I'm meant to do."

You deserve to say, *"I've got this"* And to know, deep down... you really do.

You Will Learn...

In this book, we'll explore:

★ Why your brain reacts the way it does, and how to work with it, not against it.

★ How to consistently catch yourself in the heat of a moment and consciously think through or choose a better and more *personally aligned* way forward.

★ Ways to practice and build habits that lead to more growth oriented and resilient responses.

★ Most importantly, how to model these practices in your classroom, in real time, in real life, with a real impact.

You Have Choice...

This is a thinking practice guidebook designed with one goal: To support your understanding of the power of your choice to *respond* from a place of intent, purpose, and personal alignment instead of react in habitual and unconscious ways, in your classroom, and perhaps out of the classroom too.

Your copy might be dog-eared, underlined, scribbled in, coffee stained. Maybe even glitter-covered. (We know how it is.) We hope to never see a copy of this in a secondhand bookstore — because it's too worn out, too well-loved, too useful to give away.

And although this book is short, it's not designed to be rushed through or consumed all at once. Every word, every sentence, has been chosen with care and intention. You may find yourself pausing after just a few pages, not because the ideas are complicated, but because they're deeply personal and potentially transformational. This work, strengthening your response ability, asks for reflection, practice, and patience.

It's simple, but it isn't easy.

As you move through these pages, and through your own moments of noticing, unpacking, and reworking old patterns, you'll start to see why. And by the end, you won't just understand it... you'll feel it.

It's also written with a break between certain sentences and paragraphs. When you notice these breaks, it is an invitation to pause and take a deep and intentional breath. Deep intentional breathing is the practice we use to connect our body and our brain together. More about this connection later in Chapter One.

This book is also designed to be shared. We believe deeply in the power of reflective partnerships because we've lived it.

In fact, we're pretty sure this book wouldn't even exist without the countless hours we spent in conversation about our moments in the classroom. Although we spent most of our teaching careers in separate classrooms, we discovered that many of the experiences, challenges, and emotions we faced were strikingly similar.

We learned through talking about them, reflecting on them, trying something new, and then coming back together to share what we noticed.

We validated each other's experiences.

We encouraged each other to keep going when the days were hard. And slowly, through those conversations, new ways of thinking, and responding, began to take root.

We also realized that the bond we built through our conversations became a gentle guide, helping us find our way back whenever we felt lost or couldn't recognize our own progress.

Connection itself is the support, the purpose, and the path to this transformative journey.

So, bring a friend, a co-teacher, or your whole staff into the conversation. Talk about it. Reflect. Try it out. Learn together. That's where this practice really takes root:

Within yourself.
Within a trusting relationship.
Within a caring community

You don't have to be perfect.
You don't have to stay calm all the time.
You don't have to know exactly what to say at every moment.

You **do, however**, have an opportunity to make progress and learn: **If you are willing**.

You may practice and make mistakes and practice again. You may not have all the answers, but you are working on noticing, accepting, and becoming more conscious of your choices. *Even while you make mistakes.* Because you, yes, *you*, in the middle of the busy, chaotic, beautiful classroom, are offering yourself new opportunities to grow and learn a new way of doing and being.

You already have the ability to respond with clarity, compassion, and wisdom. It lies within you. You just need to know it exists and bring it forth. You hold the **response ability**.

And this is where we begin.

Words That Matter

"I am not here to be perfect — I am here to be present."

"My pause is powerful."

"Each breath I take is a chance to begin again."

Mindful Connections

The **response ability** journey begins not with doing more, but with noticing more.

You don't have to be fixed; you just have to be **aware**.

In every messy, beautiful moment, you are not alone.

You are learning. You are growing. You are responding with intention.

Chapter 1

The Autopilot Problem

Let's start with a little honesty, shall we? There are moments in teaching, probably multiple times per day, when you're not your calmest, kindest, most composed self.

Maybe it's when a child pushes another one during a morning meeting. Maybe it's when your carefully set-up lesson falls apart before it even begins. Maybe it's when someone walks into your room, raises an eyebrow, and says, *"Wow... it's kind of loud in here..."*

In those moments, you might react. Maybe you speak sharply. Maybe you freeze or retreat inward. Maybe you say something you immediately regret. Or maybe you don't even say it out loud, you just feel it bubbling up inside: the heat, the tension, the mental *"Oh no, here we go again."* Something doesn't feel right within, but you don't know what else to do.

You're not alone. You're not broken. You are human and your brain is running on ***autopilot***.

Autopilot sneaks up on you like muscle memory. It's the reason your hand reaches for your coffee cup even when it's empty. It's why you find yourself saying, "We don't run inside!" in the exact tone your third-grade teacher used, before you even realize you opened your mouth.

When something stressful happens in your classroom, your thought brain doesn't send a polite memo to your thinking mind. It slams a big red "DO SOMETHING" button and pulls from whatever quick-fix reaction it learned long ago.

Neuroscientists have long known that the amygdala triggers fight, flight, or freeze when it senses a threat. It's a survival instinct that, while useful millennia ago, can sometimes override our best intentions in the classroom. In that split-second, your body is ready for action, even if the threat is just a spilled juice cup or a harsh look from a colleague. No analysis. No wisdom. Just speed.

And sometimes, that quick reaction *sort of* works. But more often? It leaves you feeling frustrated, disconnected, and not quite like yourself. Autopilot doesn't ask, "What would my most grounded, compassionate self do right now?" or "What can I say or do here that would help this child learn something different?" It asks, "How do we make this feeling STOP, fast?"

And that's why the real work, the brave, conscious work, is to wake up in the middle of it. To see the old script running... And remember that you have the power to write a new one.

Once you understand that *you* have the power to interrupt that automatic cycle... once you truly embrace that you can take back control of your thinking and your actions, that's when something extraordinary begins to shift.

You realize: ***You can turn off the autopilot.***

Turning off your autopilot is what we call your **response ability:** the ability to bring your conscious awareness to your intention, purpose and values.

You already have the ability to respond instead of react. It's within you. It has always been available to you but perhaps you just didn't know! So now that you do, it's time to find it, practice, and rewrite that autopilot reaction.

But first, how did you get so derailed in the first place?

Unconscious by Design...

To understand why we react the way we do, we've got to talk about your brain...not in a heavy neuroscience way, but in a *"this actually explains my Tuesday morning almost meltdown"* kind of way. So here's the deal: your brain has a default setting, and it's called **survival mode**.

For millions of years, the human nervous system has been wired to do one thing really well: **keep you alive**. It scans for threats. It prepares for battle. It reacts quickly, automatically, and unconsciously.

Thousands and thousands of years ago, those threats were real and physical: a wild animal, an unstable cliff, an approaching storm. Your brain didn't have time to analyze or reflect. You needed to *move*.

You used your senses to absorb data rapidly, and your brain stored it unconsciously for future use. Over time, those fast, automatic responses became deeply embedded patterns. And as the years go by, those processes remain in our unconscious and primal brain. Our senses are still collecting data and preparing for safety in the midst of danger.

Now fast forward to today. The "threats" look different but your brain doesn't know that.

A student throws a tantrum? ***Danger.***

A critical email hits your inbox? ***Threat detected.***

The copier breaks again, right before your observation?
ALERT MODE.

The brain doesn't ask, *"Is this actually dangerous?"* It just flips the switch: *fight, flight, or freeze.* Autopilot engaged.

Psychologists describe our brain's tendency to go on autopilot as a shortcut. One that's efficient but not always helpful. As Daniel Kahneman suggests in his work on decision-making, *Thinking Fast and Slow,* these automatic responses are fast but often bypass conscious reflection. It's like a pre-programmed loop designed for speed, not accuracy.

And before you know it, you are acting as if a hungry tiger is about to pounce on you, when all it is, is a five-year-old having a meltdown because their Lego structure broke.

That's the power of your autopilot. And that's why it's worth learning to pause, take back your **response ability**, and choose differently.

Let's go deeper.

Meet the Amygdala...

Let's zoom in on one tiny but mighty part of your brain: the amygdala. It's an almond-shaped structure nestled near your brainstem, and it's your built-in alarm system. The moment your body senses something upsetting-fear, anger, or frustration- the amygdala sends a distress signal.

Your brainstem jumps into action, prepping your body to deal with the "threat." Your muscles tense. Your breath shortens Your heart rate spikes. Your jaw tightens. It all happens so fast, you don't even notice. And then BAM, you react.

But here's the deeper layer: It's not just your brain talking to your body. Your body also sends signals back up to your brain, confirming the alarm. The tension in your shoulders? The clenched fists? The pounding heart? Your brain reads those body cues as proof that danger is real and it ramps up the reaction even more.

This creates a feedback loop: the brain signals the body, the body signals the brain, and before you know it, you're in full fight-flight-freeze mode, often over something that isn't really a threat.

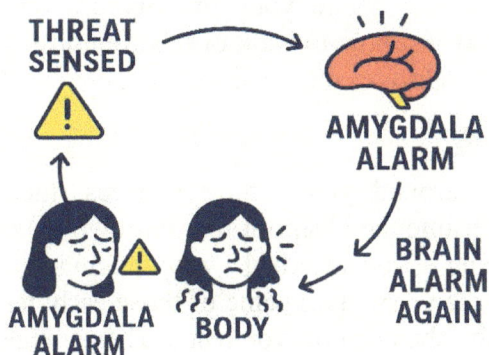

And unfortunately, those fast, automatic reactions often come with words, tones, and choices that don't reflect your best self or your most compassionate, intentional teaching practices.

It's not that you don't care. It's that your biology beats your values to the punch. But here's the big question: If it's biological, does that mean we're stuck with it? If you've come this far in the book, then you probably can guess the answer...**No!**

But first there's something else we need to face if we want to move forward: the stories we carry. In tandem with your biology, they create the unconscious reactions that cause us to feel like a victim of our circumstances instead of the author of our lives.

Beneath Our Reactions...

Before you ever spoke your first word, you were already learning. Not just how to walk or talk, but how to feel, how to cope, how to survive emotional weather.

The adults around you ...their silences, their sighs, their voices... became the blueprint for your own reactions. Without even realizing it, you absorbed a way of being in the world. And now, all these years later, some of those early lessons still live in your body, shaping how you react. They are unconscious and automatic.

Maybe, as a child, you remember the sound of a slammed cabinet door when tension filled the room. Or the long, silent car rides where no one talked after an argument. Maybe big feelings weren't talked about but instead swallowed, shoved down, or redirected with a joke and a "you're fine."

You might've learned that tears make people uncomfortable. Perhaps someone said "stop crying, that doesn't make anything better" even when your tears came from a place of empathy, sadness, or concern. As you grew older, you learned to hold back the tears, and now, feel a lump in your throat even as your eyes stay dry. A sharp reminder that the feeling still remains.

Maybe your anger was dangerous and unacceptable. You were expected to "fix your face" if you showed even the slightest disagreement with what was happening. You dug your fingernails into your palm to distract yourself from the injustice you felt all around you.

Perhaps mistakes were judged and had to be hidden or fixed quickly, instead of looked at as opportunities to learn something new and try again. You learned that consequences were something given out by the more powerful adult and felt more like punishment than something that occurred as a result of your actions. You were never taught that consequences also offered important and critical information about how to move forward.

The list goes on and on. You learned to read the room fast to keep the peace and avoid rocking the boat. You learned to stay small when things got loud, or to shout louder so you wouldn't be overpowered. You learned to hide your mistakes, or even avoid trying something new because you might fail.

That wasn't a conscious decision. That was your nervous system adapting and learning how to survive in the emotional ecosystem you were raised in. And now? Those survival strategies might still be showing up in your adult life, and especially in the classroom and school hallways where you are met head on with conflict, upset, and differences of opinion on a regular basis.

You see the loud, unpredictable circumstances of a classroom as something to be avoided or shut down instead of the opportunities for learning that they can be. So now when a child throws a tantrum, or hurls something across the room, or a parent emails you in ALL CAPS, your reaction isn't just about *this* moment. It's layered with every moment that came before it, coated with all of the lessons you absorbed about how you and others should "properly" behave.

Your body reacts and your history comes along for the ride. And if no one ever taught you how to interrupt that cycle? It just keeps looping...autopilot.

One Foundational Shift...

Let's get crystal clear on this distinction, because this is the bedrock of everything that comes next:

Reacting	Responding
Fast	Thoughtful
Habitual	Intentional
Emotionally driven	Empowered by values
Instinctual	Conscious
"Why did I do that?"	"I handled that with care."

Reacting is what happens when your brain leads with fear, frustration, or habit. Responding is what happens when your mind engages with clarity, presence, and choice.

Now, let's be real. Responding doesn't mean you never feel overwhelmed. It doesn't mean you always stay cool, calm, and collected. It simply means:

You *notice* the moment.

You *pause,* even if just for a breath.

You *accept* what's happening, instead of fighting it.

And you *choose* your next move.

That is the moment you shift from an unconscious reaction to a conscious response. That's the moment you reclaim your **response ability**. And it might not feel flashy. In fact, it might feel incredibly small. Like the breath you take when your child spills something *again* and your whole body wants to yell. Like unclenching your jaw when a colleague speaks over you in a meeting and choosing curiosity instead of sarcasm. Like walking away for a second, just so you can come back with your whole self.

These moments don't always feel powerful. Sometimes, they feel awkward. Shaky. Anticlimactic. But make no mistake, they are radical acts of reclaiming your nervous system. And this is why you'll hear us talk about taking a deep, conscious breath throughout this book.

That breath is your signal to your brain: *You are safe.* It fills your body with oxygen and is the exact opposite of your body's unconscious reaction to danger…where you hold your breath or shift into shallow, tight breathing without even realizing it.

One deep breath interrupts the brain-body feedback loop. It creates a pause. It tells your nervous system, *You don't need to fight, freeze, or flee.* And it's in that pause that you have the opportunity to make the shift: From unconscious reacting to conscious response.

Because when you choose response over reaction, you're not just shifting the outcome of that moment...You're interrupting generational patterns. As the author and theologian C.S. Lewis is often credited with saying,

"You can't go back and change the beginning, but you can start where you are and change the ending."

And that's exactly what this work is about...recognizing that every moment is a new chance to respond in a way that aligns with who you truly are. You're showing your students (and your inner child) that it's possible to feel something intense and still choose how to move forward. You're teaching by example, that power isn't loud or controlling; Sometimes, it's quiet and sometimes, it's a pause.

Sometimes, it's a single deep breath that says: *I'm here. I see this. And I'm still choosing who I want to be.* That's what makes this practice so transformative. It's not just about behavior. **It's about identity.** You're not reacting from old scripts anymore. You're responding from **your values**. And that is a whole new way of being.

Old Loop	**New Loop**
Brain: "Danger!"	Brain: "Danger!"
→ Body Tenses	→ Pause and Breathe
→ Brain Panics	→ Brain Settles
→ React	→ Respond

The Good News...

Your reactions aren't your destiny. Just because your brain has built some default settings doesn't mean you're stuck with them.

Yes, you *can* rewire your patterns. Your nervous system is able to be retrained. Your brain will learn that not every unexpected moment is an emergency.

But we also want to acknowledge this truth: For some of us, that **rewiring takes time**. It means peeling back layers of old stories, protective responses, and deeply rooted beliefs that once helped us survive, but no longer serve us now.

Repatterning isn't always a quick shift. Sometimes it takes months or even years of compassionate curiosity. Sometimes it takes looking for and building safe relationships. And sometimes, it takes the brave step of seeking support from a therapist or counselor to help us find the root of our story.

We know this is possible because we have lived it. And we also know that no matter where you start, healing is not out of reach. And when you do that for yourself, you do it for your students, too.

You model what it looks like to stay present when things get messy. You show what it means to feel big feelings without being controlled by them. **You lead not just with your lessons, but with your life.**

And the beauty of that is those moments also become your life plan. You teach, by example, that growth isn't something you preach; It's something you practice. And the most powerful part? You don't need a perfect moment to begin. You don't need a quiet room or a cleaned-up schedule or a perfect plan.

You just need one breath. One pause. One small but conscious **willingness** to do it differently. Because every time you choose presence over panic, every time you catch yourself mid-reaction and choose to soften, you are literally *changing your brain.* You're building new patterns of response.

You're teaching your body: *You are safe. Breathe. You get to choose.* And those small rewrites? They become the new story. The one where you're not stuck in old scripts. The one where your students see a grown-up who can be real *and* regulated. The one where you're leading not just from your words but from your actions.

And that? **That is the good news we all need.**

Breathe. Think. Reflect

Let's bring this home to your own life.

- **Where in your teaching life do you feel most out of control in your reactions?**

    Is it with a specific student?

    A particular time of day?

    Transitions?

    Mornings? Dismissals? Meetings?

Take a moment to name it. Write it down. Say it out loud in your car if you need to.

This isn't about judging yourself. It's about *noticing* with compassion.

Because you're not supposed to already have it all figured out. You're just supposed to be willing to look.

That's where the power begins.

Words That Matter

"My brain is doing its job and I get to choose what happens next."

"I am not my first reaction."

"I have the power to interrupt old patterns."

Mindful Connections

Understanding your brain isn't about blame; it's about clarity.

When you feel overwhelmed, remember: your brain is trying to protect you.

But your power lies
In pausing.

In choosing.

In practicing

a new response…a response that aligns with your intention and values.

One conscious moment at a time.

Chapter Two

The Moment of Choice

Let's talk about *the moment*: that tiny, almost invisible space between something happening and what you do next.

You know the one. That flicker of time after a student talks back. Or your team lead forgets (again) to include you in a decision. Or someone kindly (but unhelpfully) tells you to "just take a deep breath"... and suddenly you're breathing like a dragon.

In that split second, something flares up inside of you. Emotion rises. Your body tenses. And your brain, still doing that autopilot thing, starts whispering old scripts, old stories, old defenses."DEFEND YOURSELF. You're not being respected. You always have to do it all."

And in the blink of an eye, you're at a fork in the road. You react. **Or...**(And now you know) **You can choose to *respond*.** This is the moment we're here for. The *gap*. The pause. The breath between the stimulus and your next step. This space, even if it's only a split second, is where your true power lives. This is your ability to respond. Your **response ability** .

Wisdom of the Gap...

As Viktor Frankl, a neurologist, psychiatrist, and Holocaust survivor who founded logotherapy, wrote in his seminal work *Man's Search for Meaning,*

"Between the stimulus and response there is a space. In that space is our power to choose our response. In our response lies our growth and our freedom."

Frankl's reflections, forged in the unthinkable reality of concentration camps, underscore the profound power of choice, even in the face of the greatest adversity. In your classroom, that space between the event and your response can be the birthplace of growth for everyone in the classroom, including yourself.

Let that sink in. There is *always* a space. No matter how loud the room is, and how many unpredictable events are showing up for you. No matter how fast your senses are collecting data and telling you that you are in danger. No matter how many patterned and unconscious life stories are telling you "this is not the way people are supposed to behave…"

And in that space? Is your freedom. Your clarity. Your *choice*.

Juggle Real Life…

It's late morning. You're juggling snack time, a minor potty accident, and a child asking you if worms have bones. Then your co-teacher walks in late…again. And there it is… that *surge*. The tape starts rolling and the story in your mind is confirmed. "Why can't they be on time? Why is this always on me? "This is so unfair."

You feel the irritation rise. The story kicks in. The autopilot is ready to launch. But here, right here, is your moment. The gap.

You can react: Maybe with a glare. A cold shoulder. A sarcastic, pointed, passive-aggressive comment. Or perhaps with silent but deep seated resentment because you don't want anyone to be mad at you if you stand up for yourself.

Or, you can pause. Take one deep breath, and ask yourself: "What story am I telling myself right now?"Is it helping me? Is it true? What do I need from this exact moment? What will move us closer to clarity in our working relationship?"

The point is not to just "let it go" but to create a moment of clear communication and honesty.

You soften your body and then state your expectations and set boundaries with the words and tone that best meet your values and intention. And then remember this: how they react or choose to respond **belongs to them**. Just keep breathing.

Your response keeps *you* in alignment with yourself. It allows you to stay connected to the other person *and* to your own integrity, even as you express what's needed to keep the classroom safe and running smoothly.

It doesn't mean there won't be more conversations to have, or that their behavior will change overnight. But it *does* mean you remained grounded. And *that*, that alignment, is what moves energy forward. That's what keeps connection possible. And that difference? It shifts *everything*…for you **and** for them.

Your Inner Author…

As Brené Brown, researcher, storyteller, and author of *Rising Strong*, reminds us,

"We are the authors of our lives. We write our own daring endings."

Her words capture the essence of choice and intentionality in every moment. In your classroom, this means recognizing that each response is a line in the story you are authoring… not just for yourself, but for all of those around you.

Now let's bring that down into the micro-moments. You are the author of this breath. This moment. This choice. You hold the **pen**. Not the circumstance or the behavior in front of you, but what YOU do next. You determine that. And when you can pause long enough to remember that? You take your power back. That's where real resilience begins.

Catch the Gap...

This week, try a simple practice called **Catch the Gap**. It's not fancy. It's not complicated. But it's powerful. Here's how it works:

1. **Notice** when you feel triggered, frustrated, or reactive. Those moments when you feel your body getting tense and you begin to hold your breath.

2. **Pause** for a second.

3. **Take** a single, deep breath.
   Ask yourself:

   ★ *"What story am I telling myself right now?"*
   ★ *"Is there another way to see this?"*
   ★ *"How do I want to feel on the other side of this?"*

Then, and only then, respond. With intention. With presence. With your full **response ability**. It might be the perfect response, or it might be a response that still has some fine tuning. Either way, it will be more intentional than your unconscious reaction.

With time and practice consistently catching the gap, your actions and your intentions will start to more closely align.

Catch the Gap

Notice
the trigger

Pause
and take a breath

What story am I
telling myself?
Is there another
way to see this?
How do I want to feel

Respond
with intention

Awareness and Progress...

Here's the truth: the more you practice this, the more natural it becomes. At first, you might only catch the gap *after* the moment has passed: maybe in the car, or while brushing your teeth, or midway through your second coffee. Sometimes the gap comes, a day or two later in the middle of the night when suddenly you are wide awake and thinking about it.

That's still progress.

Because reflection builds awareness. And awareness brings forth your choices. And making that choice? That's your moment of **response ability**.

Next time, you might feel it coming. And the time after that? You might actually *pause* in the moment. Eventually, that breath becomes second nature. It becomes your new default. Not perfection. Not detachment…Just presence and choice. You are the author. You write the ending. And this moment? This one right here? **You get to choose what happens next.**

Breathe. Think. Reflect

Take a moment to reflect:

- When in your day are you most likely to react without thinking?

- What physical signals tell you that you are approaching your edge?

- What could help you remember to pause?

- How might your day feel different if you made space for even *one* thoughtful response?

Words that Matter

"I am the author of this moment."

"I choose presence over autopilot."

"I will catch the gap and respond with intention."

Mindful Connections

The **gap** between stimulus and response is where your true power lives.

Catching the gap lets you shift from unconscious reaction to conscious response.

You are not at the mercy of your first emotion or thought. You can **pause, breathe, and choose**.

Your stories (the ones your brain automatically tells) can influence your reactions but you can notice and rewrite them.

Reflection builds awareness, and awareness leads to choice.

Growth happens one breath, one pause, and one conscious choice at a time, not by being perfect, but by practicing.

Chapter Three

Presence

Before you can shift your reactions, before you can redirect your attention, and before you can show up as the teacher, leader, or human you want to be, you have to ask yourself one powerful question: **Am I actually here?** Right here? Fully. Mind, body, and spirit together. Grounded in **this** moment: not yesterday's memories and not tomorrow's worries

Presence is the beginning. Presence is the bridge. Presence is the breath.

As Eckhart Tolle, a spiritual teacher and author known for his teachings on mindfulness and presence, writes in *The Power of Now*,

"Realize deeply that the present moment is all you ever have. Make the Now the primary focus of your life."

Tolle's reflections remind us that the present is not just a fleeting moment; it is the only place where real change can happen. In the midst of classroom upheavel or the flurry of schedules, choosing to ground ourselves in *now* is a radical act of mindfulness.

The Now isn't just a nice idea. It's the only place you can ever actually choose your next step. It's the only place where real change **and** real peace, can happen.

Presence isn't something you earn after you finish the to-do list. It's not something you wait for when the classroom is quiet. Presence is a choice you make *right in the middle* of the noise. It's the foundation under your feet, even when the world feels shaky. It's the anchor when everything else is moving.

We have learned through our own work... through real, messy, imperfect days:

Presence is both the root and the bloom. The alpha and the omega. The starting line and the finish line of response ability

Practice Presence Now...

Now, let's talk about real life. **Presence happens in real time.**

Presence isn't about sitting cross-legged in a quiet room, burning sage and feeling endlessly serene. (That sounds like a really nice idea for a movie or a commercial about a yoga retreat in Bali.) But that's not the presence we are talking about. We are talking about being right here, right NOW.

Presence is: Noticing when your mind has wandered. Breathing and choosing gently to come back to the reality of this moment, even if this moment isn't serene and calm, or is causing uncomfortable feelings. And then, choosing again when you wander away...because you will.

It's noticing when you're standing in front of your students physically, but mentally scrolling through your grocery list, to do list, and tomorrow's staff meeting agenda at the same time. Or maybe that yoga retreat in Bali.

It's recognizing when you're hearing a student's voice but your internal voice is much louder saying "I can't believe they are saying THAT, in THAT tone. Who raised them?"

It's catching the gap, the pause and the breath, that lets you rejoin your life and all of the people and events in it, instead of running on unconscious momentum and story. It's intentionally choosing to **stop the judge within** and instead, stand in curiosity about the events unfolding in front of you.

Presence doesn't demand perfection.

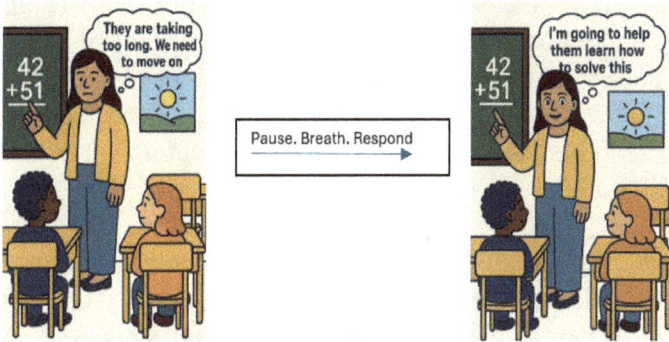

They are taking too long. We need to move on

42
+51

Pause. Breath. Respond

I'm going to help them learn how to solve this

42
+51

It simply invites return.

Real Time Presence...

It's a Thursday afternoon and you're at a mandatory team meeting. You didn't even want to be there in the first place and you have so many more important things to do. You keep thinking about the fact that most of this could have been shared in an email. You have tomorrow's activity to prepare, questions to answer, papers to grade, and you just remembered that you forgot to return that phone call.

You hear distant voices in the room. Other teachers are tossing around ideas, venting about students, arguing about next week's schedule. Suddenly someone looks at you and says, "What do you think?" And you blink. You weren't there. You realize you have no idea what they are talking about.

You nod and improvise with a "um, yah I think, so" and notice that people are looking at you with a bit of confusion. You then say, "Can you please ask the question again?" and are able to give a more accurate type of answer. After you finish, you go right back into your thoughts as you start to mentally defend not paying attention by having thoughts such as "these meetings are always too long anyway. Nobody cares about how much I have to do."

But you feel it…that hollow feeling of being absent from your own life. Of just going through the motions and wishing there was a different way. That's not failure. **That's a signal.** A call back to presence. To the now.

It doesn't mean that the staff meeting shouldn't be shorter or more organized. That's not the point. The point is, if you want to make a difference in what happens next, you have to actually BE in the moment where decisions and connections are being made. So you choose to come back. That's where **response ability** lives!

Why Presence Matters...

Presence isn't a luxury. It's a biological reset.
Here's what presence does:

* **Calms the amygdala**: You step out of unconscious panic and fear mode and into your thinking brain. That part of your brain has access to reflection, empathy, decision-making, and wisdom.

* **Interrupts old emotional patterns**: You notice your automatic story loops instead of getting caught inside them.

* **Builds trust**: With your students, your team, and yourself.

Presence is what lets you slow the story down and choose your next line, and the next chapter, intentionally.

Let's Meet Logan...

Here comes Logan with his very big personality and yes, he's testing you again. It's free choice time, and instead of building quietly, he's throwing Legos across the room. Your body wants to react. Your inner voice is speeding up: "He knows better. I told him yesterday, and the day before also. I can't deal with this today."

You feel the flush in your cheeks. You feel your breath shortening. But you catch it. You catch yourself. You remember: **Presence first. Breath deeply. Then choose.**

You place a hand on your heart, a tiny grounding move. You take one breath. You walk across the room with softness in your body. You meet Logan with presence not panic as you crouch low, soften your face, and say quietly but firmly, "I'm here. You're safe. Let's figure this out." And in that micro-moment, that barely-visible shift, you change the energy in the room. Not because Logan changed. But because you did. **You stayed with yourself**.

And that is presence in action and that is how classrooms change, one breath at a time. Presence brings you back to the moment where your choice, your clarity, and your power live.

But presence alone isn't enough. Because even when you're fully here, unless you are aware of the feeling beneath your presence, part of your mind may still be fighting against what is. The next step is one that transforms resistance into resilience: Acceptance.

Breathe. Think. Reflect

- When during your day do you feel the most disconnected or distracted?

- What are the internal signals that let you know you've left the present moment?

- What could help you return, even for one breath?

- How might your relationships shift if you practiced presence, not perfection?

Words that Matter

"I will begin again. Right now.
Even when it's loud.
Even when I feel tired.
Even when the blocks are flying."

"I am right here, right now.
And right here is enough."

Mindful Connections

Presence isn't about constant calm.

Presence is about returning, again and again, with grace and
self-compassion.

Presence brings you back to the moment, where your choice,
your clarity, and your power live.

Because the truth is:

*You are not behind. You are not broken. You are not absent.
You are just learning to come back home to yourself.
One conscious breath at a time.*

Chapter 4

Accepting What Is

Once you've returned to the moment through presence, your next step is a powerful one: accepting what is.

This chapter is about meeting the moment…not with resistance or denial, but with clarity and grounded acknowledgment. It doesn't mean you are resigning, it means you are choosing to stop fighting what's already true so you can respond from a place of power, not panic. *It's not about giving in* but **stepping in consciously**.

When you resist reality, your ability to respond gets hijacked. But when you meet the moment with steady breath and awareness, your **response ability** comes back online. Acceptance clears the emotional static. From there, you can choose with intention, strength, and clarity. **Acceptance simply means:**

"I'm not going to waste my energy fighting what's already true. I'm going to meet reality head-on, with presence and clarity, so I can choose my next step."

This shift… from resistance to presence…is *everything*. Because if you can't accept the moment, you can't respond to it. And when you stay stuck in the mental loop of "This shouldn't be happening," your nervous system goes into overdrive and at the same time your amygdala puts the brakes on. And then, your **response ability** disappears and here we go again…autopilot.

This is Happening...

Let's go back to the brain for a second. When something happens that might cause some discomfort for you...a student lashes out, a parent sends a snarky email, a colleague "forgets" to include you again...your *amygdala* is the first to react. Depending on your own personal experiences and the stories you hold as fact, your brain adjusts its level of threat alert.

It sends a flare: "This is unsafe!" "This is wrong!" "Fix it! Defend! Retreat!" Your body tightens. Your heart races. Your thoughts spiral. Why? Because your brain sees discomfort as danger. And when your nervous system perceives a threat, it doesn't want you to *accept* it, it wants you to *escape* it. But here's the problem:

When you resist reality, you lose your power to change it.

And in that moment, when your body tightens and your mind spins, you have a choice. Not always an easy one. Not always a clear one. But a choice nonetheless. You can fight the moment...or, you can feel it, breathe through it, and meet it with curiosity. Because again acceptance doesn't mean you are ignoring it. It means anchoring yourself in what *is,* so you can choose what comes *next.*

Reactivate Your Response...

Acceptance interrupts the spiral of doom. It calms your nervous system just enough to let the thinking brain back online. And you thinking brain is the part of your mind where wisdom, creativity, and clarity actually live.

Think of resistance like quicksand: The more you struggle against *what is,* the deeper you sink into frustration, blame, and overwhelm. But acceptance? That's the moment you stop flailing. It's the breath that helps you find your footing, even if it's shaky, and says: "Okay. This is happening. Maybe this isn't what I expected or planned for. But I can face it." As Eckhart Tolle, the author of *The Power of Now*, reminds us,

"Whatever the present moment contains, accept it as if you had chosen it."

Tolle's philosophy emphasizes that true power is not found in resisting reality, but in embracing it fully...just as it is. In the classroom, this radical acceptance allows you to stop fighting the challenges and start responding with clarity and purpose.

That shift doesn't mean resignation, it means *reclamation.* Only from that grounded place can you respond with clarity, direction, and real power. **Not because everything is perfect. But instead, because *you* are present. *You* are back in choice.** And *that* is where your **response ability** begins again.

When things go wrong, our internal script often sounds like this:"They should know better. I shouldn't have to deal with this. This is ridiculous. I'm so over it." These thoughts are human. Honest. *Normal.* But they don't help…They keep you stuck. Tense. Reacting instead of leading.

The shift to *"This is happening. Now what?"* is subtle but powerful. You've stopped arguing with the moment and started leading it.

This Should Not Be Happening!

FIGHTING REALITY

This is Happening. Now I Choose What is Next.

ACCEPTING REALITY

Perfectly Imperfect...

Let's look at an example from "outside" of your life in the classroom. Because let's face it, there are a lot of moments of resistance that pop up there too!

You're driving your kids to their soccer game and running late. EVERY single red light is showing up. Your phone is buzzing and you suddenly remember that YOU are responsible for the snack that day. And then, someone cuts you off and races through the yellow light in front of you and you have to slam on your brakes.

Your jaw clenches, your heart starts racing, and you open your mouth to start saying a string of unconscious phrases that you have said dozens of times at exactly the same type of moment as this. But something clicks. You hear the whisper:

"This is happening. I am here and I see this moment as it is and for what it is. I have information."

You exhale. You take another breath and say to yourself and the kids in the back "Wow, that was kind of scary for me. But we are all OK. We are going to be a little late to the game and we will handle that when we get there. But for now, let's take some deep breaths and put on some music. What shall we play?" Instead of feeding the spiral, you took some grounding breaths and put on a song.

And yes, you show up five minutes late… but not emotionally wrecked. And you find a way to stop and get fifteen small bags of chips and some juice too. It's not what you planned, but you are OK. And so is everyone in that back seat. That's the power of acceptance.

You made a choice to be in the moment. **Not perfection. Just presence.** And in that moment, you taught everyone in that car a very valuable lesson that no doubt will show up again…perhaps even one day when they get behind the wheel of a car too.

Logan Strikes Again …

Let's bring it back to Logan. It's 9:15 AM. He's already pushed over a chair, shredded the calming corner, and is yelling, "YOU'RE NOT THE BOSS OF ME!"

Your body says: "I'm done!" You feel your heart racing, you are holding your breath, and you feel like you might throw up that bagel you shoved down while driving to work this morning. Your amygdala starts showing up in full force and your stories and unconscious thoughts start pushing through to the surface:

"He should know better by now. I shouldn't have to put so much of my time and energy into this ONE child. I have other children to think about too. It's time to talk to Dad about finding a new place! He's putting me and everyone else in danger."

But you, *the practicing responder*, remember to pause and take a really deep breath. You consciously think, " Stay present. This is happening and I am going to learn as much as I can about the situation. This is an opportunity and we are not in danger. You can handle this." And you do.

You walk toward Logan, grounded and calm. You remember to soften your face as a reminder to yourself, and others, that you are present and not in any real danger." You bend down and say with a gentle but assertive tone, "You're having a hard moment Logan. I can see this must be really tough for you right now and you don't know what else to do. I'm here to help you. You're not in trouble. Let's figure this out together."

Logan pauses too, and remembers the other moments when you supported him through similar big emotions. He drops down to the ground in a heap and starts sobbing. When you go over to him, you put your hand on his back and say, "we've got this. We are going to learn a different way." And together, you do.

You're not giving up authority. You're not ignoring the behavior. You're choosing to be mindfully present, focus on what you want and accept what is, even when the situation brings up big feelings for you.

Will Logan and his big behaviors continue to show up? Probably. Because social-emotional skills like self regulation and impulse control take many events, and many "big moments" to learn. For some people it takes more time than others. So much depends on what behaviors have frequently been illuminated for them in their lives and how connected they are to others. Have they been constantly reminded of their "bad" behavior, or have there been people who have provided for and illuminated instances of success and connection with others?

You know deep down though, that he can and will learn through your presence, acceptance and belief in him. As long as you remember your ability to respond, you change the trajectory of what moves you make. Ultimately, acceptance changes the trajectory of everything that happens next.

Acceptance Is...	Acceptance Is Not...
Acknowledging what's true in the moment	Approving bad behavior
Creating space to respond instead of react	Ignoring what needs to be addressed
Choosing peace over panic	Pretending everything is okay
Meeting reality with presence and clarity	Letting people walk all over you
The foundation for strong boundaries and wise action	Being passive, weak, or checked out

Again, acceptance doesn't mean you stop caring. It means you stop fighting reality so you can meet what is happening with clarity, grace, and intention.

It's the moment where your emotional defenses soften just enough for your **response ability** to re-enter the room.

And now that you've met the moment, grounded and accepting, there's one more critical decision: Where will you place your focus? That's where we go next: learning to use conscious attention to align your actions with your intention.

Breathe. Think. Reflect

- What situations in my teaching life do I find hardest to accept?

- When do I catch myself thinking, "This isn't fair! This shouldn't be happening"?

- How does my body respond when I stop resisting, even just for a breath?

- Where could more acceptance help me reclaim peace and power?

Words that Matter

"This is happening. Now what?"

I will say it with strength.
I will say it with softness.
I will say it until it becomes a habit.

I will meet this moment with clarity and acceptance.

Mindful Connections

Peace begins the moment you stop fighting what's already true.

It doesn't mean you give up.
It means you *show up*: Fully. Calmly. Consciously.

When you practice acceptance, you make space for your
intentional and **thinking brain** to lead.

You give yourself, and your students, the gift of emotional
steadiness in the storm.

You're not here to control everything.
You're here to meet the moment with clarity, empathy,
compassion, and your **response ability**.

Chapter Five

Conscious Attention

Once you've grounded yourself in the present moment, and accepted it without resistance, something incredible opens up: **Choice.**

In every classroom moment, what you choose to pay attention to (and it IS a choice) is shaping not just how you respond, but what you're cultivating in the children, and in yourself.

This chapter invites you to use the practice of focused and conscious attention as a tool for transformation. It is noticing your thoughts, shifting your focus, and then, aligning it with what you value most. Attention, when paired with presence and acceptance, becomes your most powerful internal compass and your guiding light. And the light you shine determines what grows. Let's explore how to use it wisely.

Space For Awareness...

When you're present and accepting, you give yourself the space for awareness. And when you're aware? You get to choose what to focus on next. This is where your **response ability** lives: in your attention. As Tara Brach, a psychologist, author, and meditation teacher known for her work in mindfulness and self-compassion, reminds us,

"Thoughts are not facts. Attention is what gives them power."

Brach's work emphasizes the freedom that comes from recognizing our thoughts for what they are: temporary, shifting, and often misleading. In the classroom, this practice of noticing where your attention goes can transform your experience from reaction to mindful choice.

Because here's the truth: Your thoughts will come: unfiltered, fast, and often unhelpful and built on stories that no longer serve you. But you have a choice. You can either repeat patterned reactions based on those thoughts OR choose something different and more aligned with your deepest values, intention, and purpose. Either way, whatever you choose to focus on? That's what grows roots.

So pause for a moment and ask:

★ What exactly are you hoping for in your classroom today?

★ What are your intentions for how you teach, connect, and communicate?

★ What do you want your students to feel, practice, and remember?

If you're not sure, that's okay. But this is your invitation to stay in curiosity about your shift. **Just stay curious.** Because when intention is fuzzy and you loose sight, attention defaults to old wiring: The frustration. The assumptions. The mental checklist of everything going wrong. And when that becomes the focus? Your mindset shifting practice starts to feel like one more thing you're failing at instead of the empowering, healing practice it's meant to be.

Just. Keep. Going!

Two Light Sources...

Let's bring back what you already know from earlier: you have two powerful brain systems working at the same time.

★ Your unconscious brain, your "thought" brain, is like a **dim overhead light.**

It's always on, always buzzing in the background. It filters your reality automatically, based on old wiring: past experiences, family dynamics, cultural conditioning.

It reacts quickly without your permission and often without your awareness. It's fast, but not always accurate. Familiar, but not always true.

★ Your conscious brain or your "thinking" brain is like a **flashlight** you hold and direct in your hand.

You get to choose where to point it. This is the part of you that can pause, reflect, and **respond.** When you shine this light guided by your *values* and *intentions*, something powerful happens: You feel a deeper alignment. You come into integrity. Your body even knows. There's a sense of clarity, ease, and coherence.

But here's the catch: Even your conscious thoughts can be shaped by unconscious patterns. Sometimes what *feels* deliberate is still just the old programming wearing a new mask. That's why awareness matters. Not just the light, but the *hand holding it*, and the *why* behind where it's pointed.

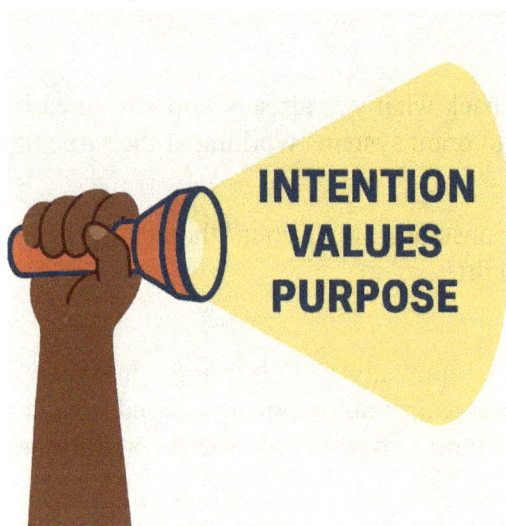

INTENTION
VALUES
PURPOSE

Light the Way...

Let's say a child knocks a stack of construction paper to the floor while trying to look for a particular color, and then walks away without picking the papers up.

Your overhead light, the unconscious brain, might automatically flick on with: "I can't believe she just did that, and just walked away." "This is so disrespectful to me and our classroom." "I can't take this kind of behavior today."

You might unconsciously have thoughts about how much this type of blatant disregard was not tolerated in the house you grew up in? Maybe you are uncomfortable with anything messy or out of line because you were taught that being clean and organized was proper or perhaps you were judged or even punished when your room wasn't clean?

Maybe you believe you think you will be judged as a poor teacher because you have a classroom that is messy and "out of control." You believe teachers should know how to control children and have a tidy classroom, because isn't that what you always saw growing up (or **thought** you saw.)

And the list goes on and on with all of the preprogrammed lessons and expectations that your brain holds on to as fact instead of a story. This behavior is upsetting the conditioned pattern that your brain is expecting to see.

But if you're present enough to notice, you can choose to redirect the flashlight, the light that is brighter and more focused than the overhead lighting in the room.

You pause, take a deep breath, and then think: "I am here to teach language, literacy, mathematics, and science not as separate from, but in partnership with, the skills of connection, problem-solving, self-regulation, and emotional understanding. These are not competing priorities; they are essential threads of the same learning experience.

I am also supporting a child's understanding of how to get along in a social group, how they can use their words and actions to uplift others, and how be part of a supportive and helpful community. These are foundational social and emotional skills and it takes many experiences over several years for children (and adults) to learn." You might even remember that you are **still learning** too.

You walk over the papers strewn all over all floor and say to everyone, "Oh my, look at the paper all over the ground. I'm going to put all of them back on the shelf so we can still use them. If anyone would like to help me, I sure could use that now."

Perhaps someone will help you pick up the paper. Maybe they won't. But the point is, your attention, your flashlight, is focusing on doing something that is beneficial and helpful to the entire classroom community, and not on the fact that the child disregarded (probably unconsciously) what she had done. The child who originally knocked them off the shelf might also notice what you are focusing on too and many times, will come over and help you as well. If they do, you can comment "look at your helpfulness here. You are also helping create a safe environment for all of us."

After you are done, you think about the child who originally created the situation. You make a mental note to focus on times when this child "is" remembering that her actions have consequences that impact the entire classroom. And THAT is the time you will choose to focus on illuminating the executive skill of perspective taking that she is developing. It's not about ignoring what's hard. **It's choosing *what you illuminate*.**

Illuminate and Strengthen…

Here is another example.

You're watching a student wander during center time and interrupt others who are already engaged. You notice the other children seem agitated by the interrupting behavior of this child. The small group you have planned during center time is still yet to begin, and all of the children who have settled into working with you are waiting. The heat is rising in your chest.

If you react from your unconscious overhead light you might say: "You need to find something to do! It's center time and there are a lot of choices for you." Or you could pause, take a deep breath, and remember your flashlight.

You remember one of your biggest and most important responsibilities is to teach children how to choose something to do and maintain focus on that activity. This is a skill that will extend far into their schooling and into their adult years. It will help them in first grade when they finish a worksheet before the rest of the students. It will help them in high school when the teacher gives them an instruction to "write a ten page essay on a topic that is important to them." It will help them in college when they have to decide on a major, or after they graduate and start looking for a job.

You also remember that this child has been having a difficult time getting into social play with others. You take a deep breath, walk over to them and say with a softened face:

"It's center time. That means it's time to make a plan. I know it can sometimes be hard to focus on something when there are so many things to do. I can help you make your own choice or help you learn how to ask to join someone else in their play. What works best for you?" When they shake their head and point at a child playing, you look at the students in the small group and gently smile "I'm going to help our friend find something to do and I will be back. You are free to make a choice as well, or you can stay and wait for me. I'll be right back."

One moment of catching the gap. One small shift. Same child but entirely different light. You just shifted from reacting to responding. You took advantage of your **response ability**! From frustration to guidance and, from "What's wrong with this kid?" to "What's the next step to help this child learn something new?"

Your flashlight can illuminate:

★ Connection
★ Self-regulation
★ Patience
★ Collaboration
★ Curiosity

And the more consistently you shine light on those things, the more you strengthen your focus on what they *can* learn and on their potential. And the more you actually focus on learning and on their potential, the more learning and skill building you bring forth!

It's all about where you put your focus; Where you choose to shine your light.

Navigate Adult Relationships...

Let's be honest, navigating relationships with other adults in a school can sometimes be trickier than managing a Kindergarten classroom on a rainy day the week before Halloween.

Some people say they have no problem with finding the gap between reaction and response in interactions with children. But interactions with adults? That's an entirely different level of *autopilot*.

Whether it's a conversation with an administrator, a tough moment with a parent or caregiver, or some tension with a co-teacher, those interactions matter. A lot. And they can activate your nervous system in ways that catch you off guard. We have expectations of how other adults "should" behave. These expectations are oftentimes **even more** embossed in our unconscious brains than our thoughts about how children should behave.

And because we're professionals (and often people-pleasers,) we've been trained, consciously or not, to stay "nice." Expectations of others vs. Expectations of ourselves. That's a rapid fire route to reaction that usually lands on resentment and frustration, mostly for ourselves.

Your old programming might whisper: "Don't make it a big deal. You're the flexible one. Just help and keep the peace." But here's the thing: Avoiding your own truth, your conscious **response ability**, doesn't build peace. It builds pressure and it reinforces old preprogrammed stories that are certainly not helpful to you or anyone else in the long run.

Every time you smile and nod while your gut is clenching and your shoulders are screaming "no," you're storing tension in your body. Your emotions sense fear, and your brain starts screaming "do something," but your unconscious programming stops you in your tracks. "Be nice." Your overhead lighting system is on, and your inner flashlight is dim. You're stepping out of alignment.

And over time, people feel that. You always feel it deeply, but so do others around you including adults AND the children you work with every day. You are giving off that certain "vibe" and others sense it without you even having to say a word.

You may be keeping things "calm" on the outside, but your inner clarity disappears and resentment builds. Your nervous system stays stuck in simmer mode, and that makes conscious response much harder to access.

Instead, try this-

Pause.

Take a deep breath.

Ask yourself:

"What's my true intention in this conversation? What do I want to illuminate here for myself **and** for them? What boundary or value matters most to me right now? **How can I use my response ability?"**

At that point, you state what you need at that moment. You respond with intention. And when your **attention** aligns with your **intention**, your words don't have to be perfect, they'll land with calm, clarity, and care.

That's where trust and connection grows. And, that's also where adult relationships will actually thrive, even when they're hard, and even when you are creating new pathways for thinking and responding.

And remember, what others do in reaction or in response to what you say belongs to them, not you. You are only in control of what YOU say and do. They are in charge of their flashlight, and you are in control of yours.

The Alignment Moment

It's Friday. You've been on your feet since 7:15 AM, mediated three debates over whose turn it is to use the magnifying glass to observe the hatching chicks, and somehow, skipped lunch. Again. You're finally packing your bag, already picturing sweatpants and silence, when the school administrator walks in with a smile you've come to recognize.

"Hey," they begin casually. "Could you stay a little later this afternoon? Just this once… we're short again in after-care." Your body feels it before your mind can name it. Tight chest. Shallow breath. The flicker of a forced smile.

And here comes the internal swirl: "I'm exhausted. Not tonight! They always ask me. If I say no, will they think I'm selfish… or not a team player?" The old scripts show up, right on cue:**Be nice. Be helpful. Don't make waves.**

But this time, something shifts. You pause. A breath. A moment. A thread of presence and acceptance. Instead of reacting from the pressure or the past, you ask yourself: "What do I really need right now? Am I able to work later (because sometimes it is possible!) **or** is this a time when I truly need to take care of myself? What version of me do I want to show up as; What pattern do I want to reinforce in myself and for others?"

You notice your attention starting to drift back toward fear... fear of being judged, guilted, misunderstood. But you catch it. And with intention, you shift. You realign with your truth, the version of you that values integrity, sustainability, and mutual respect. You soften your face. You ground your voice. And you say, gently but clearly: **"No, I'm not able to do that today."**

No apology. No over-explaining. Just truth spoken with clarity and care. It might feel wobbly at first. That's okay. Standing up for yourself often does. But this choice? It's not selfish. This is what true self-care can sound like.

It's self-honoring. It's sustainable. It's *response ability* in action.

Because boundaries are not a rejection of others. They are a commitment to stay connected to yourself. You knew you needed to take care of yourself and honored that. And when you stay connected to yourself, your presence becomes more powerful, not because you said yes, but because you said **yes to what's true for you right then**. And remember, how the other person reacts or responds to your statement is their responsibility, not yours.

That's what real leadership looks like. And that's how the classroom , and your life, begins to change.

Shine Bright Logan...

Let's bring back Logan. You've already practiced presence and acceptance, the breath, the softened face, the intentional approach. Now it's time to choose your focus.

You decide to shine your light on:

- ♥ *Emotional Regulation*
- ♥ *Task Initiation*
- ♥ *Connection*
- ♥ *Responsibility*

You remember: *You're here to teach, not control.*

So you say: "Logan, I see some materials on the floor that you were using. Are you still working with them, or are you ready to pick something new?"

He runs. You pause. You stay steady, breathe and soften. You reach for his favorite book and say: "Come sit with me for a minute. Let's read while you catch your breath." He looks at you curiously (and a bit suspiciously) at first, but then he too starts to soften as he sees you soften.

He says "okay" and comes over to settle in your lap. You put your hand on his heart and say, "Wow, I feel your heart beating so fast. Do you feel that too? Let's breathe together." And you do. You set the example and breath deeply and intentionally. You focus on your OWN breathing, not his. And then you read the book together, remember your intention, and put your attention right there.

"The materials are still on the floor. They aren't safe there and we need to do something to keep our classroom pathways clear. Do you want help putting them away, or are you able do it yourself?" He says: "Help me." So you do. Together and with presence and attention.

When you are finished you say "You did it. You put the materials back to keep our walking pathways clear and so others can find them too. That was helpful. Now your friends know where to find the Legos when they want to play with them."

Your flashlight was steady. It outshined the overhead lighting system in your brain. And look what it revealed, what a deep connection you made, and what a valuable life lesson you taught Logan AND all of those around you.

Breathe. Think. Reflect

- During stressful moments, where does my attention usually go?

- When I focus on frustration, blame, or fear, what grows?

- What values or skills do I want to see more of in my classroom?

- How can I apply conscious attention to my adult relationships too?

Words that Matter

"What I focus on, grows."

"I will focus my attention on my intention"

"I will create new pathways for thinking and responding"

(If I don't choose what to focus on, my unconscious mind will choose for me.)

Mindful Connections

Your **attention** is one of your greatest powers.

You don't have to control every moment.
You don't have to fix every behavior.
But you *do* get to **choose** where to **shine your light**.

And whatever you focus on? That's what begins to grow.

So hold your flashlight steady.
Shine it with **purpose**.
And remember...

Your influence is infinite.

Chapter 6

Building New Habits

You've paused. You've breathed. You've grounded yourself in presence, accepted what is real and shifted your attention. Now it's time to make it a habit.

Because this practice? It doesn't stop at insight. It's built in repetition. **Each moment is a choice to return**. It's built and strengthened through that return. And that's how it becomes yours...**Your peace. And your empowerment**. It's just who you are.

Response Ability Matters...

Everything you've practiced, the pause, the breath, your acceptance and your attention shift, is training your brain to respond differently. You're not just *thinking* about **response ability**: You're creating a new default, one moment at a time.

At first, it takes effort. And a clear unjudgmental lens about the process and your practices. Because the truth is, you will stumble and forget. That's how learning works. New pathways in your brain take time and repetition to build. But each intentional choice matters.

As James Clear explains in his bestselling book *Atomic Habits*,

"Every action you take is a vote for the type of person you wish to become."

Clear's work emphasizes that change is not about sudden, grand gestures but the small, intentional actions we take each day. In your classroom, each moment of presence, each breath before a response, is a vote, not just for who you are now, but for who you are becoming.

Every breath, every pause, every time you catch yourself and come back, it's a vote. A vote for the teacher, the leader, the human you already are, deep down. Because eventually, this work becomes not something you do, but who you are. Not because you changed yourself, but because you uncovered beneath the noise and the story, who you've been all along.

This is what practice does. It makes the response feel natural. It brings you home to yourself again and again.

Logan Is Learning...

Let's check in on Logan... and on you.

It's the end of the week. It's been messy, real, and exhausting. And you? You're still here. Practicing **response ability,** it seems, at every moment. SO many moments. Logan grabs a marker out of another child's hands. Tears, yelling, big movements. Logan starts to spiral like you have seen many times before. **But you don't.**

You pause. You breathe. You remember your intention and say to yourself "another chance to learn, Logan. Another chance for me. Another chance for all of us." "You start to say "Logan" but just as you start, he runs over to you, marker still in hand, and grabs your leg. You kneel down gently and say "Logan, I know you want the marker, but your friend is still using it. See his face? His face is telling us he might be feeling frustrated. Let's go over together and ask him for a turn with the marker instead of just taking it out of his hands."

Logan shrugs and walks with you to where the event took place. You put your arm around the other child and say "that looks like it might have been scary for you. You were still using that marker." The other child shakes his head. You say to the child put your hand out and tell Logan, "I'm still using the marker. You can have it when I'm finished." You say "Logan, hand the marker back. I will help you learn how to get the marker." With encouragement, Logan slowly hands the marker back and says "I want to use it." And interestingly enough after the other child shakes his head yes, Logan turns around and finds another marker to use.

Yes, he still needs support. But he's learning and practicing new skills. New skills he has never even known were available to him! And so is the other child. And so are you. **And** so are *they*...every other person in that room who saw, heard, and felt your response: The child who flinches when voices get loud, and the one who watches from the corner, quietly learning to trust her environment and social community. Your co-teacher across the room who exhaled just a little more deeply because you stayed grounded.

In moments like these, you're not just guiding Logan. You're shaping the emotional tone of the whole room. You're teaching that connection is possible, even in conflict. That repair is real and that big feelings don't have to lead to big harm. And that regulation isn't just a strategy. It's a gift you give to everyone around you.

You don't need a perfect moment to be a steady presence. You just need your flashlight on, and that belief that you can handle it. That this moment can be different. And that belief? It continues to shows up for Logan in big ways too.

In the Moment...

Choose one space in your life each day, your classroom, your home, your conversations with family or co-workers, your car ride, and consciously bring your belief in the **response ability** right there. Think about it, write it down, and tell others. At the end of the day, think about it again. How did it go?

Bring your presence. Bring your breath. Bring your acceptance. And bring your choice to return to your intention.

Shine your flashlight! The more you practice, the brighter it shines. That's how new patterns are built. It's not the great big moments but the everyday little moments that build those new pathways in your brain and patterns for your own behavior.

That's how **response ability** becomes who you are, and not just the title to this book.

Breathe. Think. Reflect

To help this practice live in your actual day (not just in theory), try checking in with yourself in small but intentional ways throughout the day.

Morning Grounding

- ♥ *What kind of energy do I want to bring today?*
- ♥ *What matters most in how I show up?*
- ♥ *Where might I need to breathe before I speak?*

Set an intention. Shine your flashlight there.

Midday Reset

- ♥ *What am I focusing on right now?*
- ♥ *What am I believing about this moment?*
- ♥ *Is there something I need to let go of so I can move forward with more peace?*

Even one breath can bring you back.

Evening Reflection

- ♥ *Where did I show up the way I wanted to?*
- ♥ *What moment taught me something?*
- ♥ *What can I forgive, release, or celebrate?*

You're not grading yourself, you're growing yourself. Growth takes time and reflection. **Accept that too!**

Words that Matter

"Even if today was hard,
response ability is still available to me.
It is always available."

"I will begin again."

"I will shine my light"

Mindful Connections

Response ability is not a skill you master and check off.
It's a *way of being* you return to.

Over and over.

With breath.
With grace and compassion for yourself.
With intention.

And even when the day is messy... even when you forget...
The light in you is still there. Let it shine.

Steady.
Soft.
Unshakable.

Chapter Seven

Conscious Choice

Let's go back to that regular Tuesday morning.

That time when the circle wasn't a circle, and no one was actually sitting. When your coffee was cold. And two children were locked in a heated battle over who was "looking at who." Tears, yelling, chaos. When your body flared up: heat in the chest, jaw tightening, that instinctive swirl of *"Do something. Now."* That time when you **almost reacted**. Almost reached for an old behavior modification tool. Almost shouted. Almost snapped.

But something inside you paused. Somehow, from out of nowhere, you actually used a different voice and acted with calmness instead of frustration and upset. And you wondered later, "what was that?" "What was happening in that moment when I actually stopped myself and did something different? I liked the way I handled that. It felt right. Could I do that again?" Yes! IF you make the choice to notice your **response ability**, time and time again.

You've always had the choice, and now, with intention and mindful practices you can walk confidently into that space whenever it shows up for you, in and out of the classroom. You've always had it, and now you know it's there.

You see the breath you took as a reset. The choice you made to be present, focus your attention, and accept the moment as a turning point. The calm you modeled was something bigger than classroom management, it was leadership. It was alignment with your intention and values. It was social-emotional learning, taught in real time, in real life.

As Simon Sinek, a leadership expert and author known for redefining what it means to lead, explains,

"Leadership is not about being in charge. It is about taking care of those in your charge."

Sinek's philosophy emphasizes that real leadership is grounded in empathy and presence. In your classroom, modeling calm and intentional responses is more than just classroom management, it's an act of mindful leadership. It shows students what it means to lead with care and clarity, moment by moment. That's what you were doing. You weren't just handling behavior, you were leading with presence and purpose. It was **response ability** in action.

The decisions you make, the ones you now think about with awareness, are conscious choices. And those choices? They're not about perfection. They're about shaping the moment in a different way... a resilient, grounded, growth-oriented way.
And now you know why. And that? That matters more than you know.

Build Deeper Connections...

You've learned how to:

Catch the gap between trigger and reaction.
Return to presence, even when it's hard.

Accept what's real, instead of resisting it.
Focus your attention where you want things to grow.

Practice... imperfectly, consistently, courageously.

You've learned how to rewire old pathways, how to soften into clarity and connection, and how to return to who you are underneath the noise. You've realized: you're not just shaping students' behavior, you're shaping their nervous systems, their beliefs about what calm looks like, and their sense of safety in the face of conflict. Never underestimate how truly powerful that is.

You are the mirror, the model and the guide. And it all starts with how *you* choose to show up...again and again.

Glimpse of Growth...

It's not always obvious. There won't always be a big high-five or a instant breakthrough. Sometimes, the change comes quietly, woven into small moments that speak volumes.

You notice that one child, the one who used to unravel at every transition, now calmly putting away their work, even offering a hand to a friend. And you catch it. You see it. A quiet flicker of growth, connection, possibility.

Or maybe it's a co-worker, the one who used to set you off with just a look, who asks you to cover their afternoon shift. And this time, instead of stewing in silent resentment or forcing a tight-lipped "sure," you take a breath, respond with grounded clarity, and feel the quiet strength of staying true to yourself.

Or maybe… the next time the circle falls apart, you smile softly, take a breath, and think: "This is the moment. This is actually a fantastic opportunity to teach and model. I've got this." That's not luck. That's not just experience. That's *practice* and that's your *choice*. That's **response ability**.

Always Remember This…

The next time you feel your nervous system firing up and jumping into your thoughts, saying: "Fix this! Say something! Hurry up!"… ***Pause***.

The next time you want to give in, shut down, or lose your way…***Pause.***

Remember what you've practiced.

Remember who you are becoming.

Remember what kind of story you want to write next, because you ARE the author.

Then choose. Because you are not broken and you are not powerless. You are not at the mercy of the moment. ***You are the one who gets to choose what happens next.*** That's your peace. That's your presence. That's your power. That's your **response ability**. *You've had it all along.*

Breathe. Think. Reflect

Ask yourself and take this with you:

- What kind of teacher, or leader, or parent, or human do I want to be when things get messy?

- How can I honor my needs, my boundaries, and my values without sacrificing my calm?

- Where and when does my light shine the brightest and how can I keep it lit?

You already have what you need.
The breath.
The pause.
The presence.
The values.
The vision.
The voice.

That's your **response ability**. *You've had it all along.*

Words That Matter

"The **response ability** is mine and I've had it all along. I'm learning how to use it one moment at a time."

Mindful Connections

This is not the end of the journey… it's the beginning of a new way of being.

You've practiced the pause. You're becoming aware of your stories, remembering who you are beneath the noise, and choosing to rewrite the scripts in your unconscious thought patterns that don't align with who you are.

Your nervous system, your thoughts, your habits… they're changing. And the impact is real: in your classroom, your conversations, your connection to self and others.

Every breath you take with intention becomes a teaching moment.
Every pause is a reclaiming of your power.
Every conscious response is a ripple that reaches far beyond the moment.

You are living the practice. You are becoming the mirror.

And your students will remember the connected and personally aligned presence you chose to offer, again and again.

Chapter Eight

A Letter For the Journey Ahead

Dear Educator,

We've said it before in this book, and we'll say it again:

The concept of knowing you have **response ability** is simple. But living it and practicing it, over and over again? Not so much.

We like to compare it to unraveling a ball of knots. It's completely doable, but it takes time, patience, and an unwavering faith that it actually is possible, even though it may seem so far away. The old stories you carry in your mind can feel unshakable.

They're so deeply woven into who you are that sometimes you can't even recognize that there's another way to see the world, your truth, and another way to *be* in the world.

The mind is a complicated place. And changing habits, especially unconscious thought habits, can be messy, slow, and incredibly brave work. *We know, because we've lived it.* In fact, it was teaching, day after day, year after year, that first pulled us toward this work.

Teaching children is what forced us to meet our own thoughts, our own patterns, our own autopilot reactions. It's what taught us that true growth doesn't start with a curriculum, it IS the curriculum. And it starts within.

If we could offer you one piece of encouragement, it would be this: **Do this work with others**. Growing and learning in connection is the heart of this work. Talk to trusted friends, family members, colleagues, mentors or even a counselor or therapist if that feels right for you. We know that opening up about your inner world is not easy. It takes vulnerability. It takes courage.

As Brené Brown reminds again in *Daring Greatly*,

"Vulnerability sounds like truth and feels like courage. Truth and courage aren't always comfortable, but they're never weakness."

Brown's research emphasizes that vulnerability is not a sign of fragility; it's the birthplace of connection and growth. In and out of the classroom, embracing this openness, whether with students, colleagues, or even with yourself, paves the way for deeper understanding and authentic relationships.

This is not a weakness. It's the foundation of growth, authenticity, and connection. The more you name your process, the more visible your **response ability** becomes, not just to others, but to yourself.

There are so many incredible voices out there…authors, teachers, and guides who have walked this path and shared their wisdom. We've included some of our favorite resources in the appendix, and we encourage you to explore them with an open heart and an open mind.

Our stories and words are just one offering, one perspective and one set of experiences among many.

We don't claim to have invented these truths. We simply hope our perspective feels like a bridge…another way to cross into your own next layer of awareness.

As you continue this work, whether for yourself, for your students, or for both, we offer one more reminder:

No curriculum, no classroom management system, no discipline plan is complete unless it starts *with you.* While so much insightful and important research on child behavior and social emotional learning has been, and continues to be, conducted, what happens at the in that classroom at the deepest level will always start *with you.*

You are the model and you are the blueprint. Your social and emotional health isn't just important for you, *it's the foundation* your students will build on every day. Children learn by watching the adults around them. They absorb far more from who we are than from what we say. The old adage "Do as I say and not as I do" is actually not possible. It's just not how human brains are wired.

So thank you for choosing to practice. (And remember it is always your *choice* to practice if you are willing.) Thank you for staying in the mess. And thank you for choosing presence, empathy, compassion, and growth not just once, but again and again. You are doing the work that matters most. And lastly, *for now,* we hope this book is just the beginning of a lifelong conversation… with yourself, with others, and with the world around you.

Stay curious and stay connected. And when in doubt? *Pause. Breathe. And Choose to Respond.*

We're in this with you…every step, every breath, every messy, beautiful moment. You've Got This!

From Our Hearts To Your Heart,

Cyndi and Paige

Appendix

Resources

The journey toward greater presence, clarity, and response ability doesn't end with the last page of this book. It's a lifelong practice. We are grateful to the many authors, researchers, and teachers who have lit the path for us with their wisdom. Below are some of the voices that have shaped and inspired our thinking. We hope these works will offer you encouragement, deeper insight, and practical tools for your own ongoing growth both inside and outside the classroom.

Mindfulness, Presence, and Emotional Awareness

Eckhart Tolle

The Power of Now: A Guide to Spiritual Enlightenment

A New Earth: Awakening to Your Life's Purpose

Thich Nhat Hanh

Peace Is Every Step: The Path of Mindfulness in Everyday Life

The Art of Communicating

Rick Hanson

Buddha's Brain: The Practical Neuroscience of Happiness, Love, and Wisdom

Tara Brach

Radical Acceptance: Embracing Your Life With the Heart of a Buddha

Radical Compassion: Learning to Love Yourself

Your World with the Practice of RAIN

Self-Compassion, Emotional Resilience, and Growth

Brené Brown

Daring Greatly: How the Courage to Be Vulnerable Transforms the Way We Live, Love, Lead

The Gifts of Imperfection: Let Go of Who You Think You're Supposed to Be and Embrace Who You Are

Kristin Neff

Self-Compassion: The Proven Power of Being Kind to Yourself

Susan David

Emotional Agility: Get Unstuck, Embrace Change, and Thrive in Work and Life

Mindful Education, Child Development, and Brain Science

Becky Bailey

Conscious Discipline: Building Resilient Classrooms

Daniel J. Siegel

The Whole-Brain Child: 12 Revolutionary Strategies to Nurture Your Child's Developing Mind

Mindsight: The New Science of Personal Transformation

Marc Brackett

Permission to Feel: Unlocking the Power of Emotions to Help Our Kids, Ourselves, and Our Society Thrive

Daniel Kahneman

Thinking, Fast and Slow

Nadine Burke Harris

The Deepest Well: Healing the Long-Term Effects of Childhood Adversity

Building Sustainable Habits and Mindful Practice

James Clear

Atomic Habits: An Easy & Proven Way to Build Good Habits and Break Bad Ones

Simon Sinek

Start with Why: How Great Leaders Inspire Everyone to Take Action

Leaders Eat Last: Why Some Teams Pull Together and Others Don't The Infinite Game

Viktor Frankl

Man's Search for Meaning

Carl Jung

Modern Man in Search of a Soul Memories, Dreams, Reflections

C.S. Lewis

The Problem of Pain

References

Brach, T. (n.d.). *Thoughts are not facts. Attention is what gives them power.* Retrieved from teachings and mindfulness practices.

Brown, B. (2012). *Daring Greatly: How the Courage to Be Vulnerable Transforms the Way We Live, Love, Parent, and Lead.* Avery Publishing.

Clear, J. (2018). *Atomic Habits: An Easy & Proven Way to Build Good Habits & Break Bad Ones.* Avery Publishing.

Frankl, V. (1946). *Man's Search for Meaning.* Beacon Press.

Jung, C. (n.d.). *The privilege of a lifetime is to become who you truly are.* Widely attributed, reflects principles of self-actualization.

Kahneman, D. (2011). *Thinking, Fast and Slow.* Farrar, Straus and Giroux.

Lewis, C.S. (n.d.). *You can't go back and change the beginning, but you can start where you are and change the ending.* Widely attributed, reflective of his philosophy on redemption and change.

Sinek, S. (n.d.). *Leadership is not about being in charge. It is about taking care of those in your charge.* Reflective of his principles on leadership and empathy.

Tolle, E. (1997). *The Power of Now: A Guide to Spiritual Enlightenment.* New World Library.

Discussion Guide

This guide is designed to deepen your understanding of the concepts presented in each chapter, with a focus on aligning responses with your truth, intention, and values. Each section includes reflection questions, alignment prompts, and practical application exercises to support mindful teaching and living.

Chapter 1: The Autopilot Problem

Reflection Questions

- When do I notice myself reacting on autopilot?

- What bodily sensations signal that I'm in reactive mode?

- How did my childhood or past environments shape my current reactions?

Alignment Prompts

- "When I feel overwhelmed, I will…"

- "The version of myself I want to respond from is…"

Practice

Keep a "reaction log" for one week. Each time you feel yourself go on autopilot, jot down the situation, your reaction, and what you wish you had done instead.

Chapter 2: The Moment of Choice

Reflection Questions

- What are my most common triggers?

- What helps me "catch the gap" between stimulus and response?

Alignment Prompts

- "In moments of stress, my intention is to…"

- "I reclaim my response ability by…"

Practice

Practice "Catch the Gap" 3 times a day. Pause. Breathe. Ask: What story am I telling myself? What else could be true?

Chapter 3: Presence

Reflection Questions

- When do I feel most disconnected during my day?

- What helps me return to the present?

Alignment Prompts

- "Being present means…"

- "When I notice I've left the moment, I will…"

Practice

Choose one recurring classroom moment (e.g., arrival, clean-up) and make it your presence practice zone. Breathe. Soften. Stay.

Chapter 4: Accepting What Is

Reflection Questions

- What situations do I struggle to accept?

- How does resistance feel in my body?

Alignment Prompts

- "This is happening. Now what?"

- "When I accept first, I gain…"

Practice

Practice naming reality out loud: "This is hard." "This is not what I wanted." Then follow with, "Now what's the next best move?"

Chapter 5: Conscious Attention

Reflection Questions

- Where does my attention usually go when I'm stressed?

- What do I most want to cultivate in my classroom?

Alignment Prompts

- I will shine my light on..."

- "What I focus on, grows. I choose to focus on..."

Practice

For one full day, consciously narrate aloud what's going well. Point out and name moments of collaboration, kindness, and effort, especially with children who challenge your intentional and aligned response most.

Chapter 6: Building New Habit

Reflection Questions

- What's one habit I want to break?

- What new habit could support my response ability?

Alignment Prompts

- "Consistency over intensity. Today I will…"

- "My response ability muscle gets stronger when I…"

Practice

Choose one micro-habit to practice (e.g., three deep breaths before responding, gratitude before dismissal) for the next 10 school days. Reflect on how it feels.

Chapter 7: Conscious Choice

Reflection Questions

- What values guide my teaching?

- How do I ensure my choices reflect those values?

Alignment Prompts

- "A conscious choice I will make tomorrow is..."

- "To stay aligned, I will..."

Practice

Write a "choice script" for a common challenge for you (e.g., a student tantrum). Include your intention, preferred words, and tone.

Chapter 8: A Letter for the Journey Ahead

Reflection Questions

- What have I learned about myself through this process?

- How has my definition of resilience or leadership changed?

Alignment Prompts

- "I now know…"

- "Going forward, I commit to…"

Practice

Write a letter to your future self. Reflect on your journey and leave reminders of what matters most. Read it when you need to remember your why.

About the Authors

Cyndi Willmarth and Paige Brown have spent nearly thirty-five years walking alongside each other in their shared journey of reflection, teaching, and personal growth. What began as simple conversations about classroom dynamics and student development evolved into a lifelong exploration of social-emotional learning not just for the children they taught, but for themselves as educators and human beings.

Cyndi holds a Bachelor of Arts in Secondary Education from the University of Illinois and a Master of Arts in Early Childhood Education from Concordia University, St. Paul. Her work in Colorado, Hawai'i and Kentucky has included teaching, coaching, and workshop facilitation. She has always been interested in whole child development, life-long learning, and has a special interest in understanding the mind, body, and spirit connection, especially as it pertains to learning.

Paige holds a Bachelor's degree in Psychology and an Elementary Teaching Certification, dedicating her career to working with elementary students in Hawai'i. Her passion extended beyond academics; she nurtured social-emotional skills, believing that helping children understand themselves and connect with others is the foundation of lifelong learning and well-being. For Paige, teaching was never just a job…it was a calling, a place where every child could feel seen, safe, and supported. Over the years, she poured her heart into helping her students grow as kind, confident, and emotionally aware individuals.

Together, Paige and Cyndi's friendship and professional bond became the heartbeat of their work. They spent countless hours exchanging ideas, supporting each other through challenges, and celebrating the joys of teaching. Their partnership is rooted in mutual respect and a shared belief in the power of reflection, connection, and authentic relationships.

Response Ability in the Classroom is their first book, and a celebration of the children who are in classrooms and the educators who give their hearts to them every day. Paige and Cyndi are on a mission to support teachers through real, practical, and heart-centered strategies. They believe every classroom moment is a chance to connect, reflect, and grow, and they invite readers to join them on this path of exploration, self-reflection, and advocacy for a more connected and compassionate learning environment.